PAPER-PIECED CURVES

8 QUILTED PROJECTS

PAPER-PIECED CURVES

8 QUILTED PROJECTS

JODIE DAVIS

Martingale
& C O M P A N Y

BOTHELL, WASHINGTON

CREDITS

President . . . . Nancy J. Martin
CEO/Publisher . . . . Daniel J. Martin
Associate Publisher . . . . Jane Hamada
Editorial Director . . . . Mary V. Green
Design and Production Manager . . . . Cheryl Stevenson
Technical Editor . . . . Laurie Baker
Copy Editor . . . . Ellen Balstad
Illustrator . . . . Laurel Strand
Photographer . . . . Brent Kane
Cover and Text Designer . . . . Trina Stahl

That Patchwork Place is an imprint of Martingale & Company.

Paper-Pieced Curves: 8 Quilted Projects
© 2000 by Jodie Davis

Martingale & Company
PO Box 118
Bothell, WA 98041-0118 USA
www.patchwork.com

Printed in China
05 04 03 02 01 00   6 5 4 3 2 1

The information in this book is presented in good faith, but no warranty is given nor results guaranteed. Since Martingale & Company has no control over choice of materials or procedures, the company assumes no responsibility for the use of this information.

Mission Statement

We are dedicated to providing quality products and service by working together to inspire creativity and to enrich the lives we touch.

Library of Congress Cataloging-in-Publication Data

Davis, Jodie.
    Paper-pieced curves : 8 quilted projects / Jodie Davis.
        p. cm.
    ISBN 1-56477-302-7
    1. Patchwork—Patterns. 2. Quilting—Patterns. I. Title.
TT835 .D3747 2000
746.46'041—dc21   99-087653

ACKNOWLEDGMENTS

✦

Many thanks to the following individuals:
My stepmom, Jayne Davis, for piecing two glorious tops—
"Robbing Peter to Pay Paul" and "Drunkard's Path";
Barbara Bunchuk for her piecing talents in "Hourglass Hexagon";
Glenda Irvine and her Thursday evening quilting class at Fort Lauderdale High School
for being the first to view the samples for this book and for receiving them with such enthusiasm;
and
last but not least, my green-feathered buddy, Indy, for not chewing up all of my pencils.

DEDICATION

✦

To Bill, for everything, but at this moment specifically, for giving me the freedom
to do what I do and must do.

Contents

PREFACE

PAPER-PIECED CURVES? Yes, you read it right, paper-pieced curves. And why not? Paper piecing with straight lines has revolutionized quilting, making painless the most detailed piecing, which most of us (especially me!) would never attempt using traditional methods. Why not take paper piecing one step further and apply it to curves?

So where did I come up with this crazy idea? While working on another paper-piecing book, I repeatedly came across curved quilt block designs in magazines and kept thinking to myself, "This could be done with paper piecing." Curves are so mundane to cut, pin, baste, and then finally sew. Couldn't some curves be paper pieced? Would it be possible to work with the little tucks that are created as a result of the excess fabric?

I couldn't resist the temptation to experiment. My first hasty trial was for a block I was designing, which included a curved window on top of a long church window. My idea worked! I drew a few practice blocks on the computer, rummaged through my stash, and headed for my sewing machine. One gorgeous Robbing Peter to Pay Paul block later, I was convinced that my technique worked.

My samples were very hurried due to my enthusiasm. When I unveiled them to my friend Glenda and her quilting class at Fort Lauderdale High School, I was thrilled that they shared my enthusiasm. In fact, they were so afraid someone else would take off and run with my idea that if it had not been so late in the evening, they would have rushed me off to the patent office.

Three short months later I sit here in our brand new home in the northern Atlanta foothills with my best quilts ever and the accompanying manuscript ready to make their way to the publisher. I've never been more excited about a book.

As my friend Glenda said with a knowing wink in my direction at her quilting class, "There **is** something new in quilting!"

INTRODUCTION

THIS IS ESSENTIALLY a project book. I start you out with the basics of paper piecing, then progress to the ins and outs of paper-piecing curves. Finishing instructions are also provided so that you have everything you need to make a complete quilt.

With these basics in hand, you're ready to jump right into the meat of the book: the eight quilts. Complete, detailed instructions guide you through the creation of several old favorites and a few new designs, all using this great technique. A difficulty rating for each quilt is provided, denoted by one (easiest) to three (challenging) spool symbols. While the paper piecing process itself, including curved paper piecing, is easy, a few of the quilts are more challenging to construct due to techniques such as inset piecing.

Finally, you won't want to miss "Resources" starting on page 76. In addition to being a frequent visitor of local quilting stores, I am always on the lookout for new mail-order resources, especially those with Web sites. These gems I share are tried and true and are sure to spark your creative muse with their wonderful offerings.

Now let's get on to those curves!

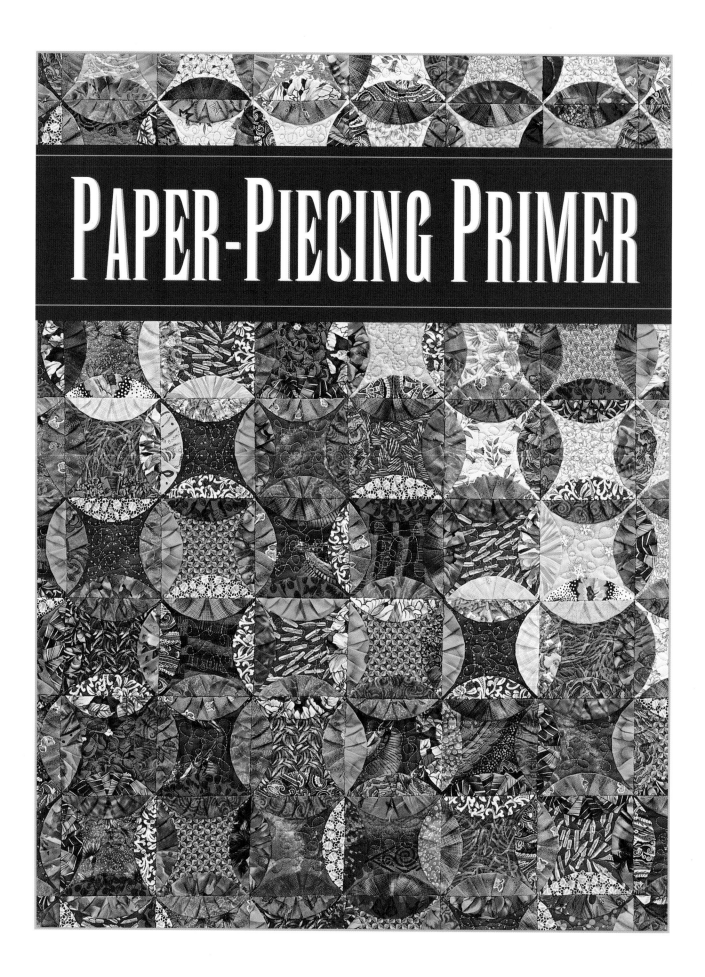

PAPER-PIECING PRIMER

Defining the Pattern Markings

THE PATTERNS for the blocks in this book are found on pages 64–75. They are full size with ¼" seam allowances added. As you look at each pattern, you will notice several things. First, each section of the pattern is numbered. The numbers indicate the sewing sequence for the fabric pieces. Second, each pattern has dashed and solid lines. Dashed lines represent cutting lines and solid lines represent sewing lines.

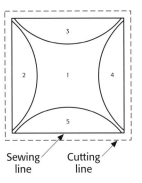

Finally, you may notice that some patterns are the mirror image of the block you see in the photo. This is because the blocks are sewn from the marked side of the paper foundation, which is the wrong side of the finished block. For symmetrical blocks, the patterns and finished blocks look the same, but for asymmetrical blocks, the finished blocks are mirror images of the patterns.

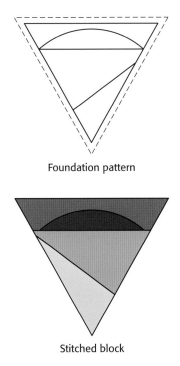

Foundation pattern

Stitched block

Selecting a Foundation Material

BLOCK PATTERNS for paper piecing are transferred to foundations. Foundations provide sewing lines and stability for sewing and piecing blocks together. They can be either permanent or temporary, depending upon the desired end result, or whether you plan to work by hand or machine.

Permanent foundations remain in the completed quilt, adding an extra layer. Because curved piecing creates folds and gathers of fabric, the added bulk of another layer—the foundation—makes a permanent foundation a poor choice for this technique. Temporary foundations, on the other hand, are removed before completing the quilt, reducing the amount of bulk in the seams and making them a good choice for curved paper piecing.

Many types of paper can be used as temporary foundations. Newsprint is the most economical, but slightly more expensive materials such as tracing paper and vellum offer important characteristics that make the additional cost worthwhile. Both are semi-transparent, allowing you to see the fabrics through the paper. This is a huge benefit when placing fabric pieces. Also, both tear away from the stitching more easily than regular paper or newsprint. You will appreciate this characteristic when the time comes to remove the paper from your blocks.

Transferring the Patterns

TO REPRODUCE the patterns, trace or photocopy them from this book onto a temporary foundation such as newsprint, tracing paper, or vellum. When tracing, use a ruler to ensure accuracy. Be sure to copy the piecing sequence numbers as well. If you choose to use a photocopy machine to reproduce the patterns, watch out for distortion. To test the precision of the copy machine, make one copy of the pattern and measure it to be sure the size matches the original. Once you finish copying the patterns, check to see if there is more than one pattern on a page. If so, cut them apart outside the dashed lines.

COLOR-CODE OR mark your patterns so that you stitch the correct fabric in the proper place in your block. When making multiple blocks, I make an extra copy of the pattern, color code it, and use it as a key so that I can easily see where the different fabrics go. You can also mark the areas on your paper foundations. For instance, on the paper foundation for the Leaf block in "Dainty Flowers," I add a *Y* for yellow in the area marked 1 and *G* for green in the areas marked 2–5.

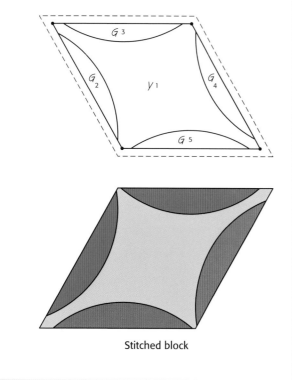

Stitched block

IT IS EASY to enlarge or reduce the patterns to create blocks in any size you desire. Simply use a copy machine with enlarging and reducing capabilities. Remember to adjust the seam allowances to ¼" by redrawing the seam allowances.

Precutting the Block Fabrics

TO MAKE paper piecing less cumbersome, I recommend precutting the fabric pieces for each section of the blocks. For your convenience, a cutting chart for block pieces is provided for each quilt. The cutting sizes are generous to ensure that the fabric pieces cover the areas in the pattern on the paper foundations. Because you trim the edges at a later time, you do not have to be as precise when cutting the fabrics for paper piecing as you do for traditional piecing. Just be sure the pieces meet the minimum measurement requirements. Yes, this wastes a bit of fabric, but in my opinion it is much better than the alternative—the dreaded seam ripper. Please be sure to cut any additional pieces, border strips, and binding strips to the *exact* measurements indicated in the project directions or in the cutting charts for these pieces.

One of the beauties of paper piecing is that the foundation stabilizes the fabrics, and as a result, it is unnecessary to follow grain-line rules strictly when cutting fabric. In normal template or rotary-cut piecing, it is imperative that the outside edges of blocks are cut on the straight of grain; if they are cut on the bias, the unstable pieces stretch and cause problems when they are pieced together. There is one caveat, however, with paper piecing. Leave your foundation (if temporary) in place until you sew your blocks together so that the fabric does not stretch. For added protection, I staystitch the outside edge of the quilt top before I remove the paper to prevent the quilt top from distorting before it is bound. Avoid the impulse to use a zigzag stitch around the outside edge. If you do, you will not be able to tear the paper out.

Preparing to Sew

SET YOUR machine for a stitch length of eighteen to twenty stitches per inch. The short stitch length creates a stronger stitch that won't come apart when tearing the paper away, and the closely spaced perforations also facilitate the tearing away of the paper.

Choose your thread according to the fabrics selected. Light gray is a good choice for lighter fabrics, while dark gray works well for black prints and darker fabrics.

Basic Paper Piecing

THE FOLLOWING is a step-by-step overview for paper piecing a block. For information about paper piecing curves, please refer to the next section, "Paper Piecing Curved Seams," on page 17. Please note that all of the blocks in this book begin with a base piece of fabric, which is referred to as piece 1. This fabric is cut to cover the area marked 1 on the pattern. Other pieces are then stitched to this background fabric.

1. Follow the cutting chart for each quilt to cut the number of pieces required for each area of the blocks. Cut each piece according to the size indicated.

2. Using a fabric gluestick, apply a dab of glue to the right side (unmarked side) of area 1 on the paper foundation. Place the background fabric (piece 1) on a flat surface, wrong side up. With the glued, unmarked side of the paper foundation facing the wrong side of the fabric, press the paper foundation in place with your hand.

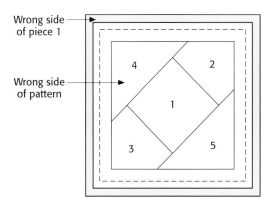

3. With right sides together, place piece 2 against piece 1 so that the majority of piece 2 is over area 1. Leave about ½" of fabric extending into the area marked 2. Working from the marked side of the foundation, stitch along the seam line between area 1 and area 2. Begin and end the stitching several stitches beyond the ends of the line.

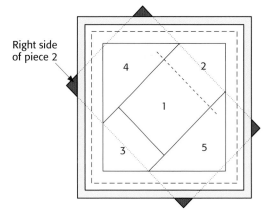

4. Flip up piece 2 to be sure it covers the area marked 2 in the pattern when it is pressed into place. Trim the seam allowance to ¼".

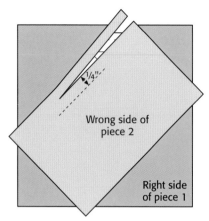

Wrong side of piece 2

¼"

Right side of piece 1

5. Fold piece 2 over the seam and press it in place.

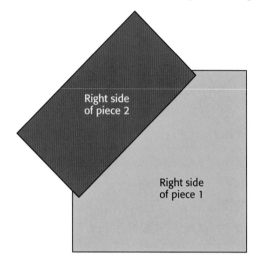

Right side of piece 2

Right side of piece 1

6. Add the remaining pieces in numerical order in the same manner.

7. Lay the block, fabric side down (marked paper foundation up), on a cutting mat. Using a rotary cutter and ruler, trim the edges of the block piece along the dashed lines. This leaves a ¼" seam allowance around the block. Make sure you cut through the paper foundation and fabric.

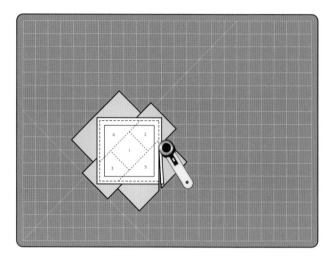

THOUGH I usually use my ¼" presser foot for all quilt-related sewing, you may find that an open-toe foot helps you see the line as you sew.

LEAVE THE paper foundation in place until after the quilt top is completed. Blocks are easier to align this way and will not become distorted by the tearing process. Also, do not worry about the grain line of the block edges. The paper foundation stabilizes the edges throughout the construction process.

WHEN PRESSING, use a hot, dry iron so that you do not distort your block. To avoid shrinking the paper foundation or getting ink from the paper foundation onto your iron and your fabric, press only on the fabric side of the blocks.

TO AVOID transferring ink from the printed pattern on the paper foundation to your ironing board cover, place a paper towel or piece of felt between the ironing board and the block.

Paper Piecing Curved Seams

HERE WE are! Actually, I feel silly explaining this technique because it is so easy. The only difference between curved and traditional, straight-line paper piecing, other than the obvious fact that you're sewing on a curved line rather than a straight line, is that because of the curved seam, the fabric can't lie flat. Therefore, the excess fabric has to be pleated. You cannot just flip the fabric back like you can in straight-line paper piecing. Pleats create great visual and textural interest on a quilt top, but they don't limit the paper-piecing technique. In fact, there is no reason why curved paper piecing cannot be used to make bed quilts. Even with the little pleats created by this technique, the quilts lie perfectly flat.

The following steps explain the process of paper piecing curves.

1. Follow steps 1–4 of "Basic Paper Piecing" on pages 15–16 to prepare the block and stitch the first 2 pieces together along the curved line. Trim the seam allowance to ¼".

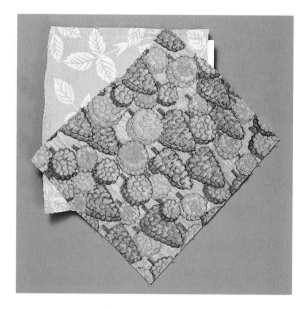

2. Fold piece 2 over the seam. Fold pleats, either toward or away from the center, into the curved fabric piece to make it lie flat. It does not matter which way you fold the fabric as long as you are consistent, folding the pleats the same way in each quilt block. Fold the pleats one at a time, placing a pin in each pleat as you go. A small curved piece with a tight curve may require 2 pleats. For a longer curve, make 4. Refer to the quilt photos for guidance.

3. Working on the marked side of the paper foundation, machine baste in the seam allowance between the solid and dashed lines to secure the tucks, removing the pins as you stitch. Use the longest stitch available; you'll be thankful later when you have to tear the stitches out to remove the paper.

4. Add any remaining pieces in numerical order in the same manner.

5. Using a rotary cutter, trim along the dashed lines.

Finishing the Quilt

ASSEMBLING THE QUILT TOP

NOW IT's time to sew the pretty blocks into a quilt top. The following steps explain how to assemble the quilt top.

1. Refer to the layout diagram for each specific quilt to arrange the finished blocks and any other required fabric pieces in the proper order. Sew them together along the outer solid line on the foundation in the order indicated in the instructions. After each seam is stitched and before it is pressed, remove the foundation paper *from the seam allowance only.* To do so, gently tear the paper as if you were tearing stamps. A gentle tug against the seam will give you a head

start in loosening the paper foundation from the stitching.

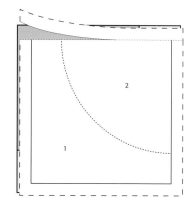

Because of the added bulk created by the pleats, stitch carefully along the pleated edges. I slow down and take one stitch at a time. To avoid bulk when stitching rows together, slow down when you get close to a seam allowance and flip the seam allowance up. Stitch right up to the seam; backstitch. Raise the needle to the up position, flip the seam allowance down, insert the needle at the point where you finished stitching, and begin stitching again on the other side of the seam allowance.

IF THERE is any doubt regarding how well the block seams will match, baste them together first. If they do not match, you only have to rip out a few basting stitches before and after the seam match to make the adjustment, then resew the entire seam with a normal stitch length.

TRY USING vinyl-coated paper clips instead of pins to hold your pieces together for stitching.

2. Remove the remaining paper foundations from the backs of the blocks.

> YOU MAY find a pair of tweezers helpful in removing the paper foundation. There are always a few pesky little tidbits of paper that remain here and there.

3. Press the completed quilt top gently, using a dry iron. Lift the iron up and down, rather than dragging it, to avoid distorting the blocks.

PREPARING FOR QUILTING

WITH THIS book I challenged myself to broaden my ability to machine quilt. Sure, I had machine quilted with my walking foot, but I decided it was time to really delve into the possibilities of free-motion quilting. Well, after a lot of practice, I must say I improved—and had fun! And I only had to tear the quilting out of one of the quilts featured in this book!

I include quilting suggestions in the project directions for each of the quilts, although you should feel free to use whatever quilting design you prefer. Now that you know what my skill level is, you can be assured that none of the quilting is too much of a challenge! Before you begin to quilt, however, you must prepare your quilt by marking the top with the quilting design and layering it with backing and batting. Follow steps 1–4 to prepare your quilt and steps 5 and 6 for quilting.

1. Mark the quilt top with the desired quilting design.

2. Cut the batting and backing 6" to 8" larger than the quilt top. This will give you 3" to 4" extra on each side of the quilt.

3. Lay the backing, wrong side up, on a flat surface. Place the batting over the backing. Center the quilt top, right side up, on top of the batting and backing.

4. Working from the center out, baste the layers of the quilt "sandwich" together with thread or safety pins.

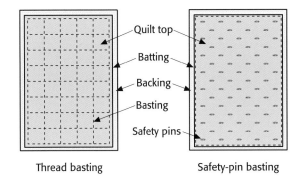

Quilt top
Batting
Backing
Basting
Safety pins

Thread basting   Safety-pin basting

> TRY ONE of the new basting sprays to hold the quilt layers together. These products temporarily hold the quilt layers together without the use of any other form of basting. Just be sure to use the spray in a well-ventilated area.

5. Quilt the top as desired or as indicated in the project directions.

6. Remove all basting stitches or any remaining safety pins when you are finished quilting.

ADDING A HANGING SLEEVE

TO HANG a quilt on a wall, sew a simple sleeve to the back. A rod or ⅜" to ¾" dowel cut 1" longer than the sleeve provides the support to hang your quilt nicely. The following steps explain how to make a hanging sleeve.

1. Cut a strip of fabric 6" wide and 1" to 2" shorter than the width of the quilt. Hem the short ends, pressing each short end under ¼" twice (½" total) and topstitching in place.

2. With wrong sides together, fold the sleeve strip in half lengthwise. Center the raw edge of the strip along the top edge of the back of the quilt. Baste it in place.

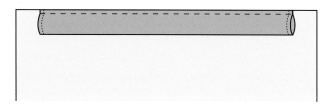

3. Stitch the binding to the quilt as instructed below, securing the sleeve in the seam.

4. Slipstitch the bottom folded edge of the sleeve to the back of the quilt, being careful not to stitch through to the front of the quilt.

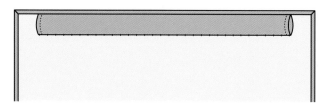

MAKING AND APPLYING BINDING

BINDING IS the last bastion of handwork remaining in quilting for those of us who embrace the sewing machine so completely. However, even though I use the sewing machine for most of my quilting, it gives me great satisfaction to sit down in the evening and actually finish my quilt by hand.

I have given widths to cut the binding strips in the instructions for each quilt. Because these quilts will not suffer heavy use like a bed quilt, I have economized on fabric by using binding strips cut on the straight of grain rather than the bias grain. The only exception is "Spinning Stars"; the binding must be cut on the bias to lie flat around the scallops. Also, if you decide to enlarge the quilts to bed size, the binding should be cut on the bias. Be sure to purchase extra fabric if you desire bias binding.

For straight-grain binding, simply cut strips from the lengthwise or crosswise grain of the fabric. Join the ends together to make one long, continuous strip.

To make bias binding, I use the flat-cut method. Make a bias cut, starting at one corner of the fabric. Then cut bias strips the desired width, measuring from the edges of the initial bias cut.

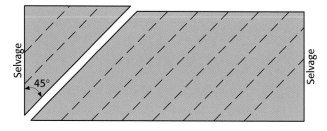

Flat-cut bias binding

Join the bias strips as shown to make one long, continuous strip. Press the seam allowances open.

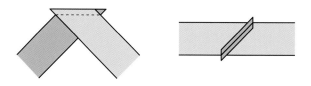

Bindings with Mitered Corners

Once you make your binding strip, this binding method that creates mitered corners is one way to attach it to your quilt. The following steps explain this process.

1. Trim the batting and backing even with the quilt top.

2. With wrong sides together, press the binding strip in half lengthwise.

3. Place the binding strip along one edge of the right side of the quilt top, matching raw edges. Leaving the first 6" or so of the binding free, stitch the binding to the quilt. Use a ¼" seam allowance. Stop stitching ¼" from the corner. Backstitch and remove the quilt from the machine.

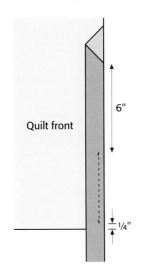

4. Turn the quilt to prepare to sew the next edge. Fold the binding up, creating a 45°-angle fold.

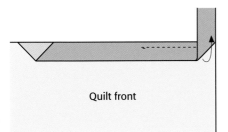

5. Fold the binding down, having the fold even with the top edge of the quilt and the raw edge aligned with the side of the quilt. Beginning at the edge, stitch the binding to the quilt, stopping ¼" from

the next corner. Backstitch and remove the quilt from the machine. Continue the folding and stitching process for the remaining corners.

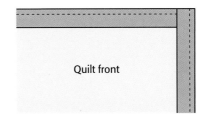

6. When you are within approximately 4" of the starting point, stop stitching. Cut the binding end so it overlaps the unstitched binding at the beginning by at least 5". Pin the ends together 3½" from the starting point. Clip the binding raw edges at the pin mark, being careful not to cut past the seam allowance or into the quilt layers. Open up the binding and match the ends as shown. Stitch the ends together on the diagonal.

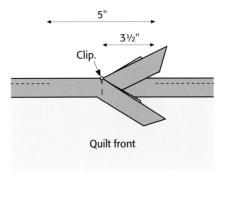

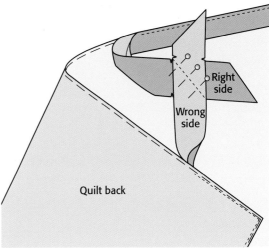

7. Refold the binding, and check to be sure that it fits the quilt. Trim off the binding tails and finish stitching the binding to the edge.

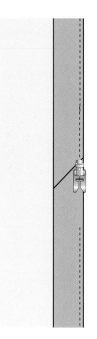

8. Fold the binding to the back of the quilt over the raw edges of the quilt "sandwich," covering the machine stitching. Slipstitch the binding in place, mitering the corners.

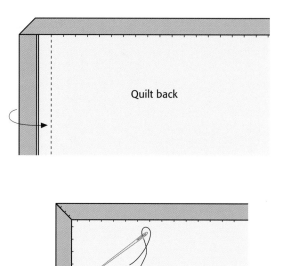

Quilt back

Quilt back

The Quilts

Robbing Peter to Pay Paul

ROBBING PETER TO PAY PAUL, *pieced by Jayne Davis, 1999, Boynton Beach, Florida, 48" x 48".*
Designed and quilted by Jodie Davis.

SCRAPPY LOOKING QUILTS *are a lot of fun to make, and the scrappier they are, the better. The trick is not to match your fabrics too closely; otherwise, the quilt looks contrived. If you examine this quilt, you will see that the fabrics certainly do not match. The variety of textures and print size is exactly what gives this quilt such pizzazz. For that extra shot of zing, add red, yellow, and orange prints and place them at the edges and within the body of the quilt to act as highlights.*

Finished quilt size: 48" x 48"
Finished block size: 4" x 4"
Difficulty rating:

Materials

42"-wide fabric

- 1½ yds. *total* of assorted light blue prints
- 1½ yds. *total* of assorted dark blue prints
- 4½ yds. *total* of assorted medium blue prints
- ⅞ yd. *total* of assorted bright color prints
- 54" x 54" square of batting
- 3 yds. of fabric for backing
- ½ yd. of fabric for binding*

* The binding will not be visible on the front of the quilt.

Directions

1. Refer to "Transferring the Patterns" on pages 13–14 to prepare 144 paper foundations of the Robbing Peter to Pay Paul pattern on page 64.

2. Cut the fabric pieces for each block as indicated in the cutting chart.

CUTTING CHART FOR BLOCK PIECES

Refer to "Precutting the Block Fabrics" on pages 14–15 before you cut the pieces for each block.

Fabric	No. of Pieces to Cut	Dimensions	Piece Number
Light Blue	78	5" x 5"	1
Dark Blue	66	5" x 5"	1
Medium Blue	500	2½" x 5"	2–5
Brights	76	2½" x 5"	2–5

3. Refer to step 2 in "Basic Paper Piecing" on page 15 to glue the paper foundations to each piece 1. Each piece 1 is either light blue or dark blue.

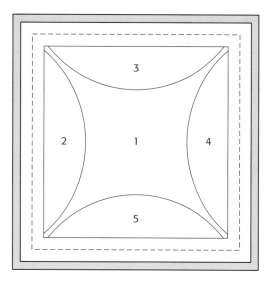

4. Following the instructions in "Paper Piecing Curved Seams" on pages 17–18, stitch pieces 2–5 to each foundation to make the following blocks:

   ♦ 36 blocks, each with light blue background fabric, 3 medium blue curved pieces, and 1 bright curved piece

   ♦ 3 blocks, each with light blue background fabric, 2 medium blue curved pieces, and 2 bright curved pieces

   ♦ 31 blocks, each with dark blue background fabric, 3 medium blue curved pieces, and 1 bright curved piece

   ♦ 1 block with dark blue background fabric, 2 medium blue curved pieces, and 2 bright curved pieces

   Paper piece each of the remaining 73 blocks—39 with light blue backgrounds and 34 with dark blue backgrounds—with 4 medium blue curved pieces each.

5. Refer to the quilt layout diagram to stitch the blocks into rows. Remove the paper from the seam allowances after stitching each seam. Press

the seam allowances open. Stitch the rows together. Remove the paper from the seam allowances. Press the seam allowances open.

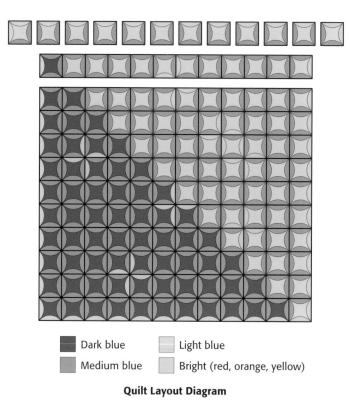

| ■ Dark blue | □ Light blue |
| ■ Medium blue | ▨ Bright (red, orange, yellow) |

Quilt Layout Diagram

6. Remove the remaining paper foundations.

7. Layer the quilt top with batting and backing, following the instructions in "Preparing for Quilting" on page 19.

8. Quilt a simple, free-form loopy design on the background fabrics. This will emphasize the three-dimensional effect of the curved paper piecing.

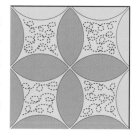

9. To bind the quilt, cut six 2¼"-wide strips across the width of the fabric. Join them together, following the instructions in "Making and Applying Binding" on page 20. From the pieced strip, cut 2 strips, each 48" long; and 2 strips, each 52" long. Press the strips in half lengthwise, wrong sides together.

10. With the binding raw edges aligned with the quilt raw edges, stitch the 48"-long strips to the quilt sides. Trim the ends even with the top and bottom edges of the quilt. Press the binding strips away from the quilt.

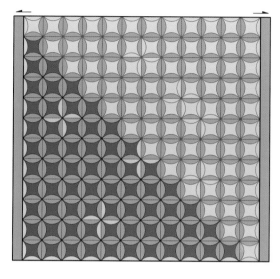

11. Center the 52"-long binding strips on the top and bottom edges of the quilt, leaving 2" extending at each end. Starting ¼" from the corner of the quilt, stitch the binding in place. Do not stitch through the side bindings. Press the binding strips away from the quilt.

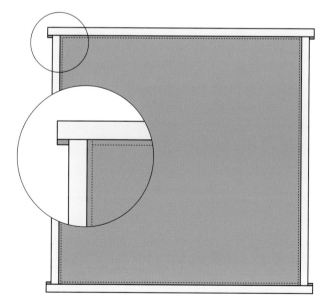

12. Fold the side binding strips to the back of the quilt so that no binding shows on the front. Pin, then slipstitch the binding in place.

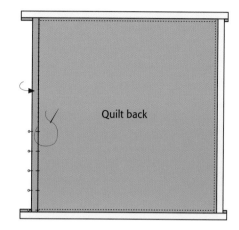

Quilt back

13. Fold under the extra 2" at the ends of the top and bottom bindings, enclosing the corners. Fold the binding strips to the back of the quilt so that no binding shows on the front, and slipstitch them in place.

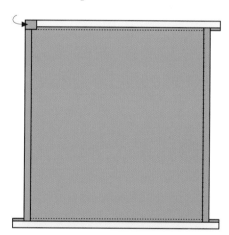

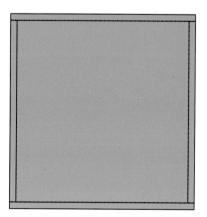

Drunkard's Path

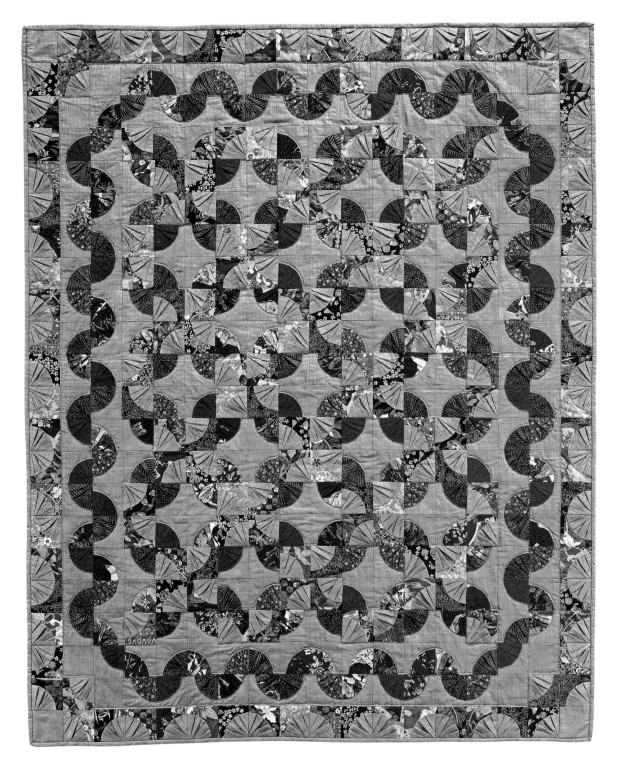

DRUNKARD'S PATH, *pieced by Jayne Davis, 1999, Boynton Beach, Florida, 55" x 67".*
Designed and quilted by Jodie Davis.

THIS OLD FAVORITE *gets a new twist when you use curved paper piecing. I was planning to make this quilt with traditional fabric choices until an online shopping spree veered me decidedly off course. The rich gold background of this quilt is the perfect foil for the delicious red and blue Japanese prints that form the "path."*

Finished quilt size: 55" x 67"
Finished block size: 12" x 12"
Difficulty rating:

Materials
42"-wide fabric

- 5⅝ yds. of gold print
- ½ yd. *each* of 6 assorted red prints
- ½ yd. *each* of 6 assorted blue prints
- 62" x 73" piece of batting
- 3½ yds. of fabric for backing
- ½ yd. of fabric for binding

Directions

1. Refer to "Transferring the Patterns" on pages 13–14 to prepare 384 paper foundations of the Drunkard's Path pattern on page 65.

2. Cut the fabric pieces for the border blocks and binding exactly according to the sizes in the cutting chart for additional pieces and binding. From the remaining fabrics, cut the pieces for each block as indicated in the cutting chart for block pieces.

3. Refer to step 2 in "Basic Paper Piecing" on page 15 to glue the paper foundations to each piece 1. Each piece 1 is either gold or blue.

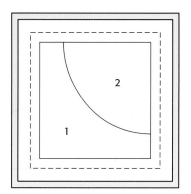

CUTTING CHART FOR ADDITIONAL PIECES AND BINDING

Fabric	No. of Pieces to Cut	Dimensions	Location
Gold	12	3½" x 3½"	Border blocks
	6	2½" x 42"	Binding

CUTTING CHART FOR BLOCK PIECES

Refer to "Precutting the Block Fabrics" on pages 14–15 before you cut the pieces for each block.

Fabric	No. of Pieces to Cut	Dimensions	Piece Number
Gold	212	4" x 4"	1
	172	4½" x 4½"	2
Blue	172	4" x 4"	1
Red	212	4½" x 4½"	2

4. Following the instructions in "Paper Piecing Curved Seams" on pages 17–18, stitch piece 2, which is either gold or red, to the foundations to make the following blocks:

   ♦ 212 blocks with gold background fabric and 1 red curved piece
   ♦ 172 blocks with blue background fabric and 1 gold curved piece

5. Stitch 16 paper-pieced blocks together as shown to make each of the Drunkard's Path blocks. Make 12 blocks. Remove the paper from the seam allowances after stitching each seam.

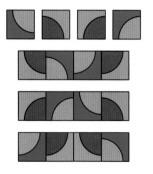

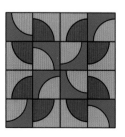

Make 12.

6. Use the remaining paper-pieced blocks to make the borders shown below. Stitch the blocks into rows, then stitch the rows together. Remove the paper from the seam allowances after stitching each seam.

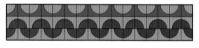

Side borders
Make 2.

Top and bottom borders
Make 2.

7. Refer to the quilt layout diagram to stitch the blocks into 4 rows of 3 blocks each. Stitch the rows together. Remove the paper from the seam allowances after stitching each seam.

Quilt Layout Diagram

8. Stitch the side borders to the sides of the quilt. Press the seam allowances toward the borders.

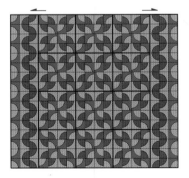

9. Stitch the top and bottom borders to the top and bottom edges of the quilt. Press the seam allowances toward the borders.

10. Remove the remaining paper foundations.

11. Layer the quilt top with batting and backing, following the instructions in "Preparing for Quilting" on page 19.

12. Outline quilt the background section of each block with a gold background as shown.

13. Stitch the binding strips together, following the instructions in "Making and Applying Binding" on page 20.

14. Following "Bindings with Mitered Corners" on pages 20–22, bind the quilt.

Hearts and Gizzards

Hearts and Gizzards *by Jodie Davis, 1999, Canton, Georgia, 34" x 34".*

I ABSOLUTELY LOVE *real red fabrics, but they are not easy to find. So, whenever I spot a true red fabric, I snatch it up.*

For this quilt, group your fabrics into darks and lights. A red with white dots is a dark, whereas a white or pink with red dots is a light. Do not be too concerned if one fabric spans the two categories; that is what makes a quilt interesting.

Finished quilt size: 48" x 48"
Finished block size: 4" x 4"
Difficulty rating:

Materials

42"-wide fabric

- ⅜ yd. *each* of 7 assorted dark red prints
- ⅜ yd. *each* of 6 pink prints
- 40" x 40" square of batting
- 1¼ yds. of fabric for backing
- ⅓ yd. of fabric for binding

Directions

1. Refer to "Transferring the Patterns" on pages 13–14 to prepare 144 paper foundations of the Hearts and Gizzards pattern on page 65.

2. Cut the pieces for each block as indicated in the cutting chart.

CUTTING CHART FOR BLOCK PIECES

Refer to "Precutting the Block Fabrics" on pages 14–15 before you cut the pieces for each block.

Fabric	No. of Pieces to Cut	Dimensions	Piece Number
Dark red	112	3½" x 7"	1
	64	3" x 3"	2–3
Pink	32	3½" x 7"	1
	224	3" x 3"	2–3

3. Refer to step 2 in "Basic Paper Piecing" on page 15 to glue the paper foundations to each piece 1. Each piece 1 is either pink or dark red.

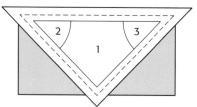

4. Following the instructions in "Paper Piecing Curved Seams" on pages 17–18, stitch pieces 2 and 3 to each foundation. Match the pink curved pieces with the dark red backgrounds and the dark red curved pieces with the pink backgrounds.

5. Stitch together 20 blocks with 4 dark red background pieces, and 16 blocks with 2 pink and 2 dark red background pieces each, as shown. Remove the paper from the seam allowances after stitching each seam. Press the seams open.

Make 20.   Make 16.

6. Refer to the quilt layout diagram to stitch the blocks into 6 rows of 6 blocks each. Stitch the rows together. Remove the paper from the seam allowances after stitching each seam. Press the seams open.

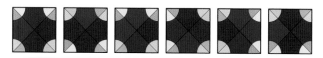

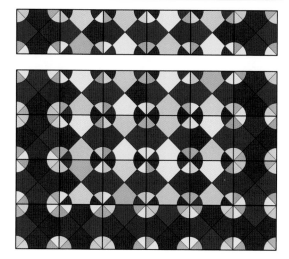

Quilt Layout Diagram

7. Layer the quilt top with batting and backing, following the instructions in "Preparing for Quilting" on page 19.

8. Quilt around the circle that is created when the curved pieces meet. Add a free-form wave pattern around each circle.

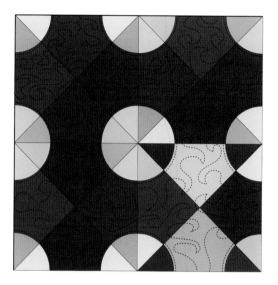

9. From the binding fabric, cut four 2½"-wide strips across the width of the fabric. Stitch the strips together, following the instructions in "Making and Applying Binding" on page 20.

10. Following "Bindings with Mitered Corners" on pages 20–22, bind the quilt.

Spinning Stars

SPINNING STARS *by Jodie Davis, 1999, Canton, Georgia, 40" x 50".*

THE INSPIRATION FOR *the color choices for this quilt came from a photo I cut out of a magazine, just waiting for the right project to come along. Can you tell that I like clear, bold colors?*

Finished quilt size: 40" x 50"
Finished block size: 9½" x 9½"
Difficulty rating:

Materials

42"-wide fabric

- 3¼ yds. *total* of 6 assorted green prints
- ¼ yd. *each* of 6 assorted blue prints
- ¼ yd. *each* of 6 assorted red prints
- ¼ yd. *each* of 6 assorted yellow prints
- ¼ yd. *each* of 6 assorted orange prints
- 46" x 56" piece of batting
- 2¾ yds. of fabric for backing
- ½ yd. of fabric for binding
- Freezer paper for piecing scalloped outer border

Directions

1. Refer to "Transferring the Patterns" on pages 13–14 to prepare 24 paper foundations each of the left, center, and right units of the Spinning Stars pattern on pages 66–68.

2. Cut the inner and outer border pieces exactly according to the sizes in the cutting chart for border pieces. From the remaining fabric, cut the pieces for each block as indicated in the cutting chart for block pieces.

CUTTING CHART FOR BORDER PIECES

Fabric	No. of Pieces to Cut	Dimensions	Location
Green	58	1¾" x 2½"	Inner border
	36	4" x 6"	Outer border (Triangles)
Blue, Red, Yellow, Orange	60	1¾" x 2½"	Inner border
Blue, Red, Yellow, Orange	32	5" x 6"	Outer border (Scallops)

CUTTING CHART FOR BLOCK PIECES

Refer to "Precutting the Block Fabrics" on pages 14–15 before you cut the pieces for each block.

Fabric	No. of Pieces to Cut	Dimensions	Piece Number
Green	144	3½" x 7"	1 and 3
Blue, Red, Yellow, Orange	144 (total)	3½" x 7"	2 and 4

3. Refer to step 2 in "Basic Paper Piecing" on page 15 to glue the paper foundations to each piece 1.

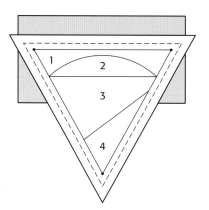

4. Following the instructions in "Paper Piecing Curved Seams" on pages 17–18, stitch piece 2 to each foundation. Refer to "Basic Paper Piecing" on pages 15–17 to stitch pieces 3 and 4 to each foundation.

5. Stitch a left, center, and right unit together as shown, matching raw edges and dots. Remove the paper in the seam allowances. Press the seam allowances to one side. Make 24. Stitch 2 pieced units together to make a block. Remove the paper

in the seam allowances. Press the seam allowances open. Make 12.

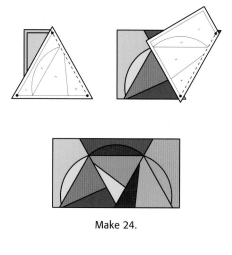

Make 24.

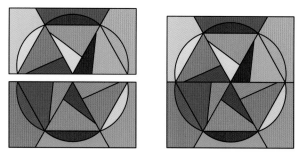

Make 12.

6. Refer to the quilt layout diagram to stitch the blocks into 4 rows of 3 blocks each. Stitch the rows together. Remove the paper from the seam allowances after stitching each seam. Press the seam allowances open.

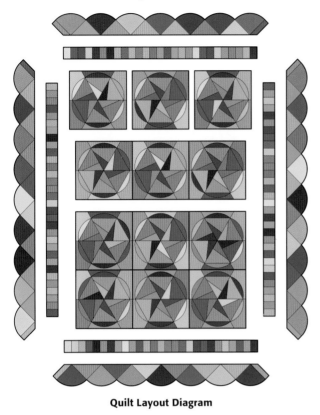

Quilt Layout Diagram

7. To make one of the inner side border strips, stitch 16 green and 16 bright color (blue, red, yellow, orange) 1¾" x 2½" rectangles together. Alternate the bright color rectangles with the green rectangles. Begin and end the strip with a bright color rectangle. Press the seam allowances to one side. Make 2 strips. Stitch these strips to the sides of the quilt as shown in the upper right diagram. Press the seam allowances toward the borders.

8. In the same manner described in step 7, make the inner top and bottom borders by stitching 13 green and 14 bright color (blue, red, yellow, orange) rectangles together. Press the seam allowances to one side. Make 2 strips. Stitch these inner borders to the top and bottom edges of the quilt. Press the seam allowances toward the borders.

9. Remove the remaining paper foundations from the back of the blocks.

10. To make the outer borders, trace the pattern on page 69 onto the paper side, not the shiny side, of the freezer paper. Repeat the pattern as necessary to complete the required number of triangles and scallops. For the outer side borders, trace 10 triangles and 9 scallops, beginning and ending with a triangle. Make 2 strips. For the outer top and bottom borders, trace 8 triangles and 7 scallops, beginning and ending with a triangle. Make 2 strips.

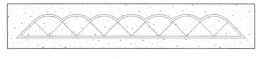

Top and bottom borders
Make 2.

Side borders
Make 2.

11. Refer to "Basic Paper Piecing" on pages 15–17 for general information on how to paper piece the outer border pieces to the freezer-paper strips. Start with a green piece (4" x 6") for the first triangle on the pattern. Next, choose a red, yellow, blue, or orange piece (5" x 6") for the scallop. Continue stitching these outer border pieces to the freezer-paper strips, alternating the green pieces for the triangles with the red, yellow, blue, and orange pieces for the scallops. Trim the strips along the dashed lines.

12. Mark the center of each outer border strip, the quilt sides, and the quilt top and bottom edges. Pin the outer side border strips to the quilt sides, matching centers. Stitch, beginning and ending ¼" from the inner border corner. Repeat for the top and bottom borders.

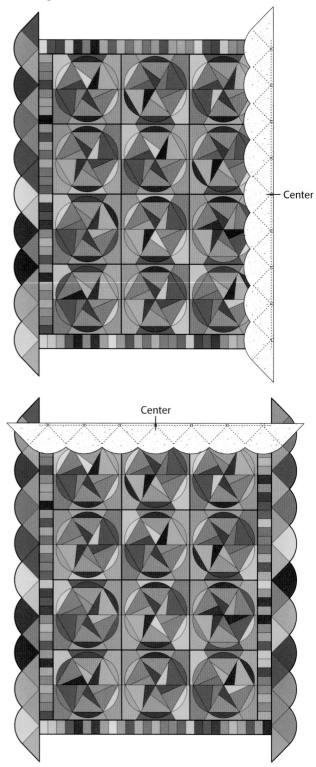

13. To miter the outer border corners, fold the quilt diagonally with right sides together, matching the triangles at the end of the borders. Mark a 45° angle from the point where the stitching ends. Stitch along the marked line. Trim the seam allowance to ¼", then press it to one side. Repeat for the remaining corners.

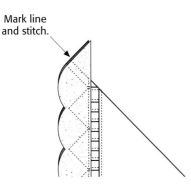

Mark line and stitch.

14. Remove the paper foundations from the outer border.

15. Layer the quilt top with batting and backing, following the instructions in "Preparing for Quilting" on page 19.

16. Quilt close to the seam line around the pieces that form the stars in the center of each block. Stitch just outside the curved crescents to form a circle, and on each side of the pieced inner border.

17. Following the instructions in "Making and Applying Binding" on page 20, make 6 yards of bias binding.

18. With the quilt and binding raw edges aligned, stitch the binding to the quilt, beginning on one side of a curve. When you reach an inside corner of a curve, leave the needle in the fabric, turn the quilt, rearrange the binding, lower the presser foot, and continue sewing. Be careful not to stretch the binding as you sew.

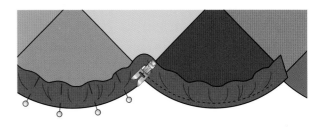

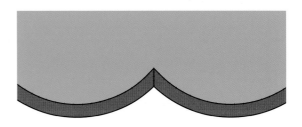

19. Fold the binding to the back of the quilt, one scallop at a time. A miter will form at the inside point as you move from one scallop to the next. Pin, then blind stitch the binding in place.

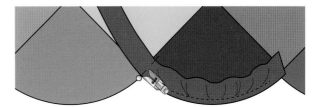

Crescent Moon Dance

CRESCENT MOON DANCE *by Jodie Davis, 1999, Canton, Georgia, 38" x 38".*

Batiks against black *make this quilt highly effective. Though the curved paper piecing is easy, the set-in seams used to sew the blocks into a quilt top make this quilt a bit more challenging.*

Finished quilt size: 38" x 38"

Finished block sizes:

BLOCK A: 4" x 4"

BLOCK B: 4" x 6"

BLOCK C: 6" x 6"

Difficulty rating:

Materials

42"-wide fabric

- 1⅞ yds. of solid black
- ¼ yd. of yellow batik
- ¼ yd. of orange batik
- ⅜ yd. of red batik
- ⅜ yd. of purple batik
- ⅜ yd. of blue batik
- ¼ yd. of green batik
- 45" x 45" square of batting
- 1¼ yds. of fabric for backing
- ½ yd. of fabric for binding

Directions

1. Refer to "Transferring the Patterns" on pages 13–14 to prepare 64 paper foundations of the Crescent Moon Dance pattern on page 70.

2. Cut pieces for the block squares and rectangles, borders, and binding exactly according to the sizes in the cutting chart for additional pieces, borders, and binding. From the remaining fabric, cut the pieces for each block as indicated in the cutting chart for block pieces.

3. Refer to step 2 in "Basic Paper Piecing" on page 15 to glue the paper foundations to each piece 1. Each piece 1 is black and 3½" x 5".

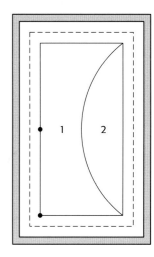

CUTTING CHART FOR ADDITIONAL PIECES, BORDERS, AND BINDING

Fabric	No. of Pieces to Cut	Dimensions	Piece Number
Solid black	16	2½" x 4½"	Blocks A and B
	9	2½" x 2½"	Block C
	2	2" x 26½"	Inner border
	2	2" x 29½"	Inner border
	2	3½" x 31½"	Outer border
	2	3½" x 37½"	Outer border
	4	2½" x 42"	Binding
Yellow batik	2	1½" x 9½"	Middle border
	2	1½" x 8½"	Middle border
Orange batik	2	1½" x 7"	Middle border
Red batik	2	1½" x 7"	Middle border
Purple batik	2	1½" x 9½"	Middle border
	2	1½" x 8½"	Middle border
Blue batik	2	1½" x 7"	Middle border
Green batik	2	1½" x 7"	Middle border

CUTTING CHART FOR BLOCK PIECES

Refer to "Precutting the Block Fabrics" on pages 14–15 before you cut the pieces for each block.

Fabric	No. of Pieces to Cut	Dimensions	Piece Number
Black	64	3½" x 5"	1
Yellow batik	8	3½" x 5"	2
Orange batik	8	3½" x 5"	2
Red batik	12	3½" x 5"	2
Purple batik	16	3½" x 5"	2
Blue batik	12	3½" x 5"	2
Green batik	8	3½" x 5"	2

4. Following the instructions in "Paper Piecing Curved Seams" on pages 17–18, stitch a batik piece 2 to each foundation.

5. Referring to the quilt layout diagram below for color placement, stitch 1 paper-pieced block to 1 black 2½" x 4½" rectangle, right sides together, to make Block A. Make 4. Remove the paper from the seam allowances after stitching each seam. Press the seam allowances open.

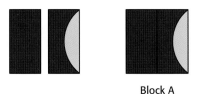

Block A
Make 4.

6. Referring to the quilt layout diagram below for color placement, stitch 2 paper-pieced blocks to 1 black 2½" x 4½" rectangle, right sides together, to make Block B. Make 12. Remove the paper from the seam allowances after stitching each seam. Press the seam allowances open.

Block B
Make 12.

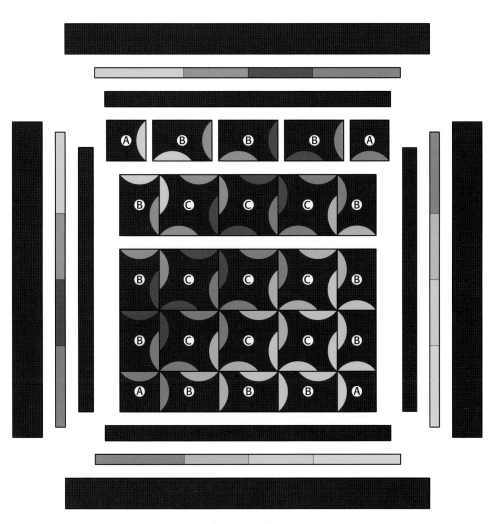

Quilt Layout Diagram

7. Referring to the quilt layout diagram for color placement, make Block C by sewing 4 paper-pieced blocks to 1 black 2½" x 2½" square as shown, backstitching at the dots. Make 9. Remove the paper from the seam allowances after stitching each seam. Press the seam allowances open.

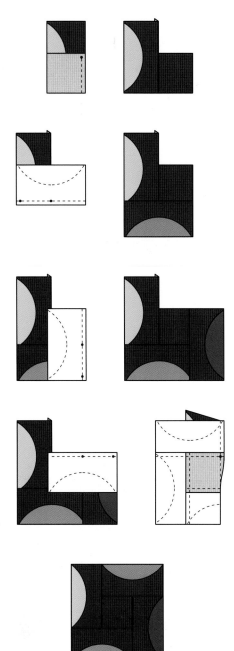

Block C
Make 9.

8. Refer to the quilt layout diagram to stitch the blocks into 5 rows of 5 blocks each. Make 2 rows with 2 of Block A and 3 of Block B, and 3 rows with 2 of Block A and 3 of Block C. Stitch the rows together. Remove the paper from the seam allowances after stitching each seam.

9. Stitch the black 2" x 26½" inner border strips to the sides of the quilt. Press the seam allowances toward the borders. Sew the remaining 2" x 29½" inner border strips to the top and bottom edges. Press the seam allowances toward the borders. Remove the paper from the seam allowances after stitching each seam.

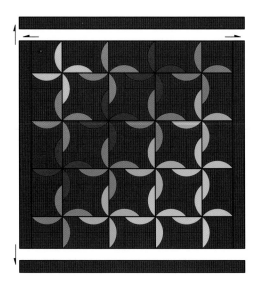

10. Remove the remaining paper foundations.

11. To assemble the pieces for the middle border strips, refer to the following border assembly diagrams. Stitch the border pieces together as shown, paying close attention to the lengths and colors. Press the seam allowances to one side. Next, stitch a middle border strip to each side of the quilt, aligning the strip colors with the block colors. Press the seam allowances toward the borders. In the same manner, align and stitch the top and bottom border strips to the top and bottom edges of the quilt. Press the seam allowances toward the borders.

8½"	7"	7"	8½"

Left border

8½"	7"	7"	8½"

Right border

9½"	7"	7"	9½"

Top border

9½"	7"	7"	9½"

Bottom border

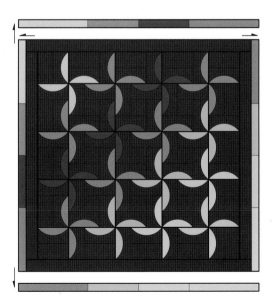

12. Stitch the 3½" x 31½" outer border strips to the quilt sides. Press the seam allowances toward the outer borders. Stitch the remaining outer border strips to the top and bottom edges. Press the seam allowances toward the outer borders.

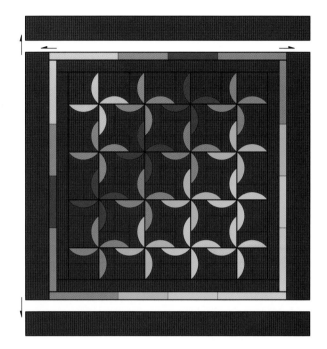

13. Layer the quilt top with batting and backing, following the instructions in "Preparing for Quilting" on page 19.

14. Quilt the blocks and borders as desired with the template provided on page 70.

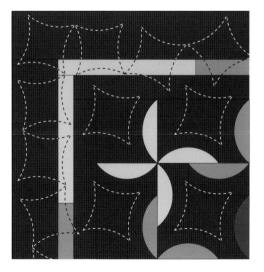

15. Bind the quilt, following "Bindings with Mitered Corners" on pages 20–22.

Dainty Flowers

DAINTY FLOWERS *by Jodie Davis, 1999, Canton, Georgia, 44½" x 44½".*

LOOK CAREFULLY AND *you can see that this arrangement mimics a Tumbling Blocks pattern. Bursting with multiple designs like a kaleidoscope, this exciting quilt brings any room to life.*

Finished quilt size: 44½" x 44½"

Difficulty rating:

Materials
42"-wide fabric

+ 3 yds. *total* of assorted yellow prints and gold prints
+ ¼ yd. *each* of 7 assorted purple floral prints and blue floral prints
+ ⅜ yd. *each* of 6 assorted green prints
+ 50" x 50" square of batting
+ 2¾ yds. of fabric for backing
+ ½ yd. of fabric for binding

Directions

1. Refer to "Transferring the Patterns" on pages 13–14 to prepare 42 paper foundations of the Flower pattern and 30 paper foundations of the Leaf pattern on pages 71–72.

2. Cut the pieces for each block as indicated in the cutting chart for block pieces.

3. Refer to step 2 in "Basic Paper Piecing" on page 15 to glue the paper foundations to each piece 1. Each piece 1 is either yellow or gold.

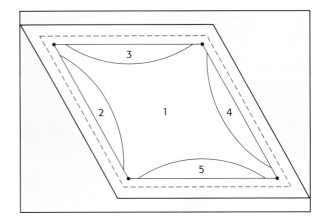

CUTTING CHART FOR BLOCK PIECES

Refer to "Precutting the Block Fabrics" on pages 14–15 before you cut the pieces for each block.

Fabric	No. of Pieces to Cut	Dimensions	Piece Number
Yellow, Gold	72 (total)	6" x 9"	1 (Flower and Leaf)
Blue, Purple	12 from *each* fabric	3½" x 5"	2–3 (Flower)
Green	120	3½" x 5"	2–5 (Leaf)

4. Following the instructions in "Paper Piecing Curved Seams" on pages 17–18, stitch the green Leaf block pieces 2–5 to the Leaf pattern foundations.

5. Following the instructions in "Paper Piecing Curved Seams" on pages 17–18, stitch the Flower block pieces that are numbered 2 and 3 and are either purple or blue to the Flower pattern foundations. For each Flower block, use the same color of fabric for pieces 2 and 3.

6. "Dainty Flowers" consists of 7 Flower units. Each unit is made with 6 matching Flower blocks. To piece each Flower unit, stitch 3 matching Flower blocks together as shown. Remove the paper from the seam allowances after stitching each seam. Press the seam allowances to one side. Repeat these steps to stitch the remaining 3 matching Flower blocks together. Stitch the 2 sets of 3 matching blocks together. Remove the paper from the seam allowances after stitching each seam. Press the seam allowance open. Make 7 Flower units.

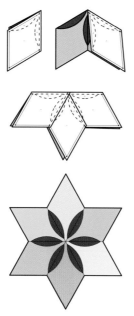

Make 7.

7. Refer to the quilt layout diagram to arrange the Flower units and Leaf blocks. Beginning with the center Flower unit, stitch the Leaf blocks to each "petal" between the dots; backstitch at the dots. Remove the paper from the seam allowances after stitching each seam. Press the seams open.

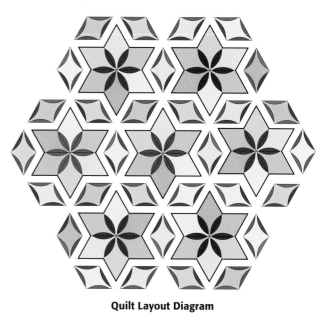

Quilt Layout Diagram

8. Continue stitching the Leaf blocks and Flower units together. Stitch the outer Leaf blocks to the quilt last. Remove the remaining paper foundations.

9. Layer the quilt top with batting and backing, following the instructions in "Preparing for Quilting" on page 19.

10. Use a meandering stitch to quilt the yellow and gold areas.

11. To bind the quilt, cut four 2½"-wide strips across the width of the fabric. Join them together, following the instructions in "Making and Applying Binding" on page 20. Apply the binding to the quilt, following "Bindings with Mitered Corners" on pages 20–22. At each inside corner, stitch ¼" past the corner; backstitch. Clip the binding and the quilt raw edge to the stitching. Readjust the quilt and binding and begin stitching again as close as you can get to the point where you left off. Backstitch and continue stitching.

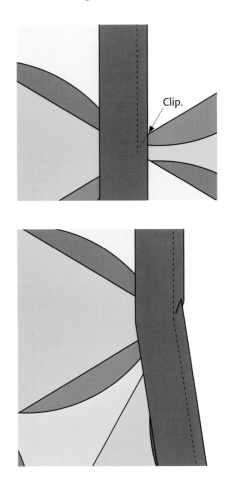

Clip.

Hourglass Hexagon

HOURGLASS HEXAGON, *pieced by Barbara Bunchuk, 1999, Fort Lauderdale, Florida, 35½" x 47".*
Designed and quilted by Jodie Davis.

A VARIETY OF COLOR *combinations can be used with this quilt design. Try this one out: replace the beige background fabrics with greens and jewel-tone fabrics for the curved patches. You will suddenly find yourself in a garden full of flitting butterflies!*

Finished quilt size: 35½" x 47"

Difficulty rating:

Materials

42"-wide fabric

- ¼ yd. *each* of 10 beige prints
- ⅜ yd. *each* of 5 brown and/or black plaids
- ⅞ yd. of brown print
- 2⅜ yds. of large-print fabric for the outer border and binding
- 44" x 55" piece of batting
- 2 yds. of fabric for backing
- ½ yd. of fabric for binding

Directions

1. Refer to "Transferring the Patterns" on pages 13–14 to prepare 180 paper foundations of the Hourglass Hexagon pieced triangle pattern on page 73.

2. Cut the pieces for the plain triangles, half triangles, corner pieces, borders, and binding exactly according to the sizes in the cutting chart for additional pieces, borders, and binding. The templates for the outer border corner piece, half triangle, and plain triangle are on page 73. From the remaining fabric, cut the pieces for each block as indicated in the cutting chart for block pieces.

3. Refer to step 2 in "Basic Paper Piecing" on page 15 to glue the paper foundations to each beige piece 1.

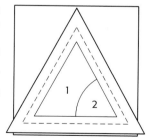

53

CUTTING CHART FOR ADDITIONAL PIECES, BORDERS, AND BINDING

Fabric	No. of Pieces to Cut	Dimensions	Location
Beige prints	90	Plain triangle	Rows
Brown print	30	Plain triangle	Rows
	24 (reverse 12)	Half triangle	Sides
Brown/black plaids	7	1½" x 5"	Inner border
Border print	2	6½" x 42½"	Outer border
	2	6½" x 64½"	Outer border
	5	2½" x 42"	Binding
	4 (reverse 2)	Corner	Outer border

CUTTING CHART FOR BLOCK PIECES

Refer to "Precutting the Block Fabrics" on pages 14–15 before you cut the pieces for each block.

Fabric	No. of Pieces to Cut	Dimensions	Piece Number
Beiges	18 from *each* fabric	4½" x 4½"	1
Brown/black plaids	36 from *each* fabric	3" x 3"	2

4. Following the instructions in "Paper Piecing Curved Seams" on pages 17–18, stitch a plaid piece 2 to each block foundation.

5. Referring to the quilt layout diagram, stitch the pieced, plain, and half triangles into rows. Stitch the rows together. Remove the paper from the seam allowances after stitching each seam.

Quilt Layout Diagram

6. Stitch the plaid inner border strips together to form one long strip. Press the seam allowances to one side.

7. Measure the straight sides of the quilt. From the pieced inner border strip, cut 2 strips 2" to 4" longer than the sides of the quilt. Stitch the strips to the quilt sides. Press the seam allowances toward the borders. Repeat for the top and bottom of the quilt.

8. Place the remaining inner border strip piece along the edge of one of the angled corners; stitch. Trim the excess fabric even with the top and side borders. Repeat for the remaining 3 corners. Press the seam allowances toward the borders.

9. Stitch the outer border corner pieces to the angled edges of the quilt. Press the seam allowances toward the borders.

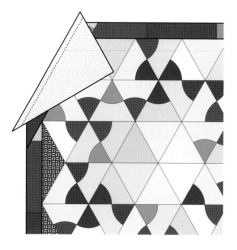

10. Remove the remaining paper foundations.

11. Stitch the 6½" x 64½" outer border strips to the quilt sides. Press the seam allowances toward the borders.

12. Stitch the remaining outer border strips to the top and bottom edges of the quilt. Press the seam allowances toward the borders.

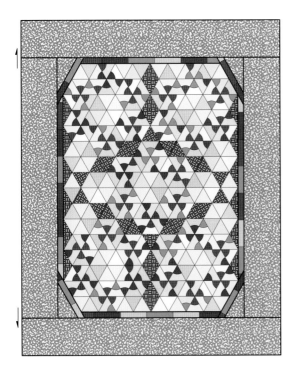

13. Layer the quilt top with batting and backing, following the instructions in "Preparing for Quilting" on page 19.

14. Outline quilt the dark pieces as illustrated. Free-motion quilt in the border as desired.

15. Bind the quilt, following "Bindings with Mitered Corners" on pages 20–22.

Diamond Star

DIAMOND STAR *by Jodie Davis, 1999, Canton, Georgia, 29" x 29".*

Because I do *not like to fuss with traditional curved piecing, I thought I would never get to make this block design that I cut from a magazine years ago. When the idea for curved paper piecing struck me, I recalled this block, dug up the clipping, and made it.*

Finished quilt size: 29" x 29"
Finished block size: 10¼" x 10¼"
Difficulty rating:

Materials
42"-wide fabric

- 42"-wide fabric
- 2¼ yds. tone-on-tone white or off-white print
- Assorted prints: ¼ yd. *each* of 1 red, 1 blue, 1 green, and 1 yellow for the Diamond blocks, Small and Corner Sashing Square blocks, and Prairie Point border
- Assorted prints: ⅛ yard *each* of 1 red, 1 blue, 1 green, 1 yellow, 2 orange, 2 purple, and 2 pink for the Small and Corner Sashing Square blocks and Prairie Point border
- 34" x 34" square of batting
- 1 yd. of fabric for backing
- ¼ yd. of fabric for binding

Directions

1. Refer to "Transferring the Patterns" on pages 13–14 to prepare 24 paper foundations of the Diamond pattern, 72 paper foundations of the Small Sashing Square pattern, and 9 paper foundations of the Large Sashing Square pattern, all on page 74.

2. Cut pieces for the setting triangles and squares, borders, and binding exactly according to the sizes in the cutting chart for additional pieces, border, and binding. The templates for the setting triangles and setting squares are on page 75. From the remaining fabric, cut the pieces for each paper-pieced block as indicated in the cutting chart for block pieces.

CUTTING CHART FOR ADDITIONAL PIECES, BORDER, AND BINDING

Fabric	No. of Pieces to Cut	Dimensions/Template Name	Location
White/Off-white	16	Setting triangle	Blocks
	16	Setting square	Blocks
Assorted prints	68	3" x 3"	Border
Binding Fabric	4	2½" x 42"	Binding

CUTTING CHART FOR BLOCK PIECES

Refer to "Precutting the Block Fabrics" on pages 14–15 before you cut the pieces for each block.

Fabric	No. of Pieces to Cut	Dimensions	Piece Number
White/Off-white	32	2½" x 3½"	2–3 (Diamond)
	288	2" x 3½"	2–5 (Small Sashing Square)
	36	2" x 3"	2–5 (Large Sashing Square)
1 Red, 1 Blue, 1 Green, 1 Red	8 of *each* color	2" x 3½"	1 (Diamond)
	16 of *each* color	2" x 2"	4–5 (Diamond)
Assorted prints	72	2¼" x 2¼"	1 (Small Sashing Square)
	9	3" x 3"	2–3 (Large Sashing Square)

3. Refer to step 2 in "Basic Paper Piecing" on page 15 to glue the paper foundations with the Diamond pattern to each Diamond block piece 1. Each piece 1 for the Diamond block is red, blue, green, or yellow.

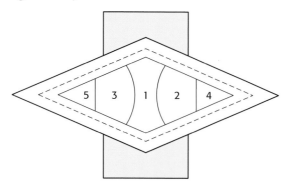

4. Following the instructions in "Paper Piecing Curved Seams" on pages 17–18, stitch the Diamond block pieces 2 and 3 to the Diamond pattern foundations.

5. Follow the instructions in "Basic Paper Piecing" on page 15 to stitch Diamond block pieces 4 and 5 to the Diamond pattern foundations. Use the same color of fabric for pieces 1, 4, and 5 on each of the Diamond pattern foundations. Make 8 paper-pieced Diamond blocks from each of the 4 colors of fabric.

6. To piece the Diamond blocks into a star, stitch 2 matching paper-pieced blocks, right sides together, along one edge. Remove the paper from the seam allowance after stitching the seam. Press the seam allowances to one side. Make 4. Stitch 2 pairs together to make half of a star. Remove the paper from the seam allowance after stitching the seam. Press the seam allowances to one side. Make 2. Stitch 2 halves of a star together to complete a star. Remove the paper from the seam allowance after stitching the seam. Press the seam allowance open. Repeat for the remaining 3 colors.

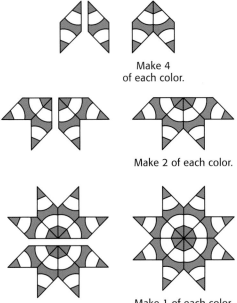

Make 4
of each color.

Make 2 of each color.

Make 1 of each color.

7. With right sides together and raw edges aligned, stitch one edge of a setting square to a corner edge of a star. Start stitching ¼" from the outer edge. At the inside corner, stop stitching ¼" from the edge of the square; backstitch. Match the adjacent edge of the setting square to the adjacent edge of the star. Stitch together in the same manner. Repeat for the remaining 3 corners.

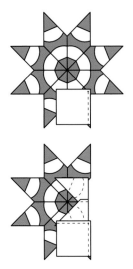

8. Stitch the setting triangles into the top, side and bottom openings in the same manner as the setting squares in step 7 to make a complete Star block. Press the set-in seams toward the Diamond blocks.

9. Refer to "Basic Paper Piecing" on pages 15–17 to paper piece the Small Sashing Square blocks and Large Sashing Square blocks. For these blocks, assorted prints are used for piece 1, and pieces 2–5 are cut from the white/off-white fabrics.

10. To make the top, middle, and bottom sashing strips, stitch 3 paper-pieced Large Sashing Square blocks and 12 paper-pieced Small Sashing Square blocks together as shown. Make 3. To make the side sashing strips, stitch the remaining Small Sashing Square blocks into strips of 6 squares each. Make 6. Remove the paper from the seam allowances after stitching each seam.

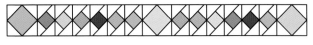

Make 3.

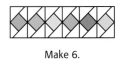

Make 6.

11. Alternately stitch 2 blocks and 3 side sashing strips together, beginning and ending with a sashing strip. Make 2 rows. Remove the paper from the seam allowances after stitching each seam.

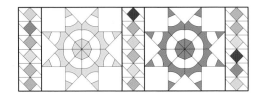

12. Refer to the quilt layout diagram to stitch the rows together with the top, center, and bottom sashing strips as shown.

Quilt Layout Diagram

13. Remove the remaining paper foundations.

14. Layer the quilt top with batting and backing, following the instructions in "Preparing for Quilting" on page 19.

15. Use a meandering stipple stitch to quilt the white/off-white areas of the quilt.

16. To make the Prairie Point border, fold each 3" x 3" border square in half to form a triangle. Fold them in half again to make Prairie Points; press. Pin a Prairie Point to a corner of the quilt, aligning the raw edge with the edge of the quilt top. Insert the next Prairie Point into the folds of the first, making sure the open folds face the same direction. Pin the Prairie Point in place. Continue adding Prairie Points across the edge until you have a total of 17. Adjust the spacing as necessary. Repeat for the remaining 3 sides of the quilt top. Baste the Prairie Points in place.

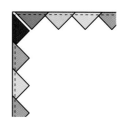

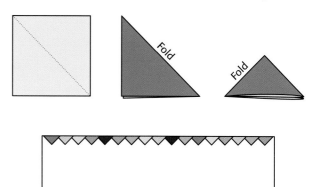

17. Press the binding strips in half lengthwise, wrong sides together. Stitch a binding strip to one side of the quilt top, matching the raw edges of the quilt, Prairie Point border, and binding. Repeat for the opposite side of the quilt top. Trim the ends even with the quilt top and bottom. Press the binding strips away from the quilt.

18. Stitch the remaining 2 binding strips to the top and bottom of the quilt top, starting ¼" from the corners. Trim the ends 2" beyond the edges of the quilt top. Do not stitch through the side bindings.

19. Fold the side binding strips to the back of the quilt so that no binding shows on the front of the quilt. Pin, then slipstitch the binding in place.

Back of quilt

20. Fold under the 2"-long ends on both the top and bottom bindings, enclosing the corners.

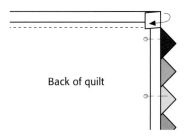

Back of quilt

21. Fold the binding strips to the back of the quilt and slipstitch them in place.

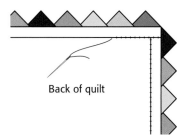

Back of quilt

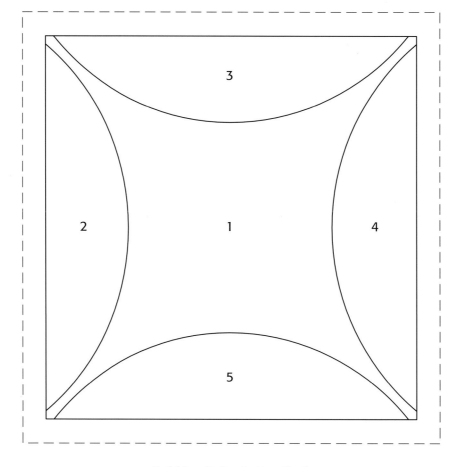

Robbing Peter to Pay Paul

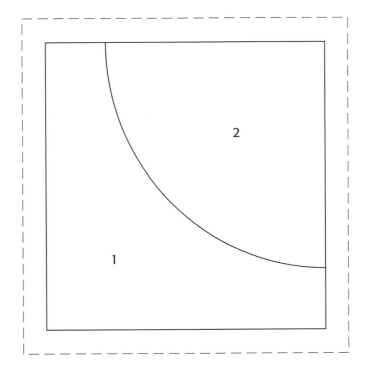

Drunkard's Path

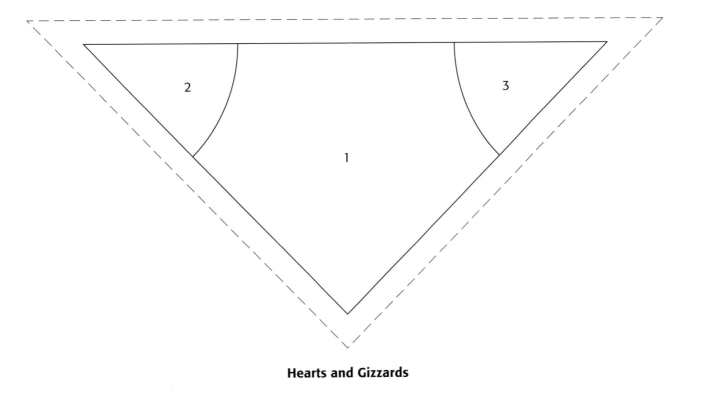

Hearts and Gizzards

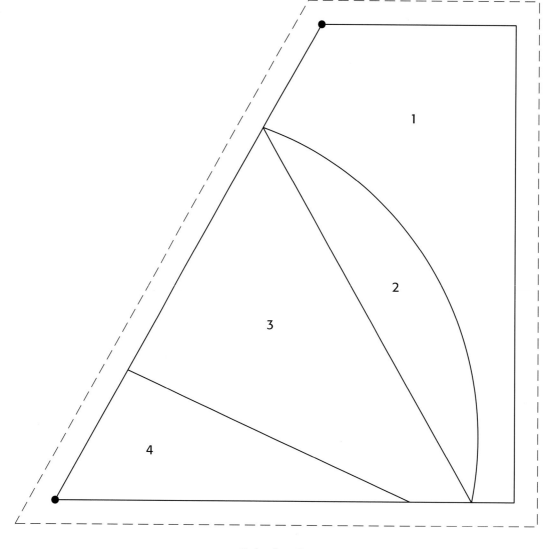

Spinning Stars
Left Unit

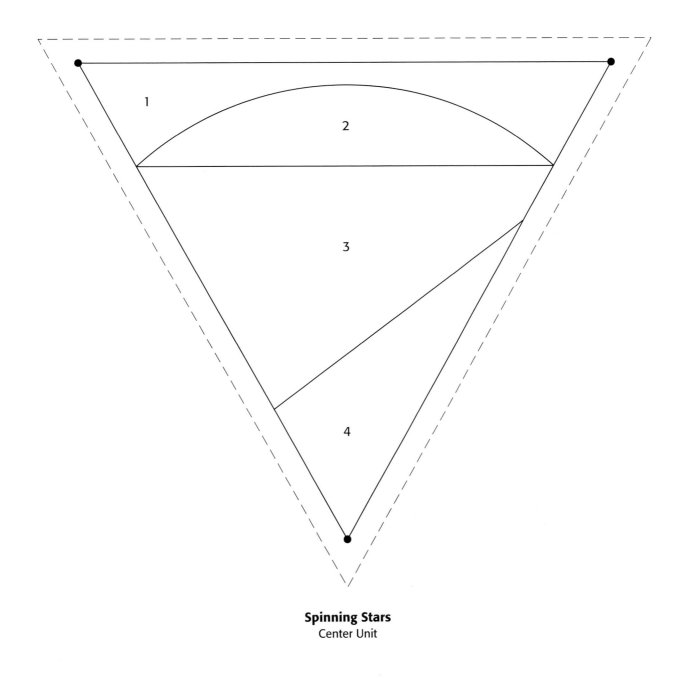

Spinning Stars
Center Unit

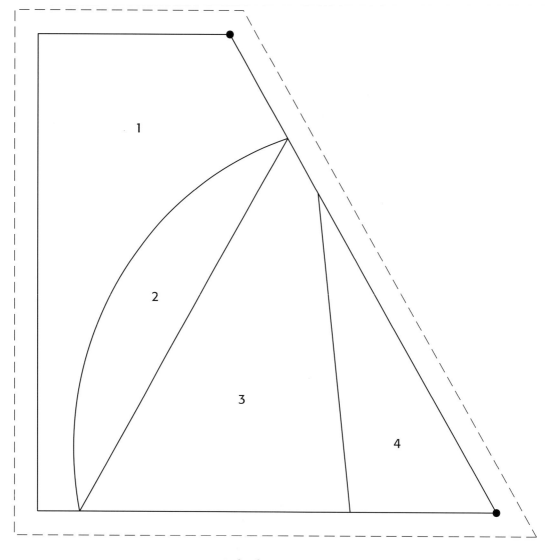

Spinning Stars
Right Unit

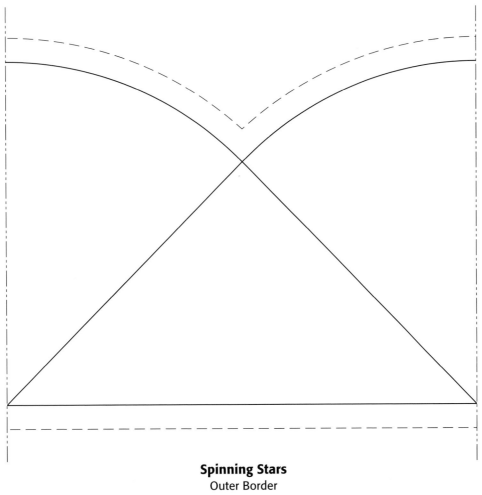

Spinning Stars
Outer Border
Pattern Repeat

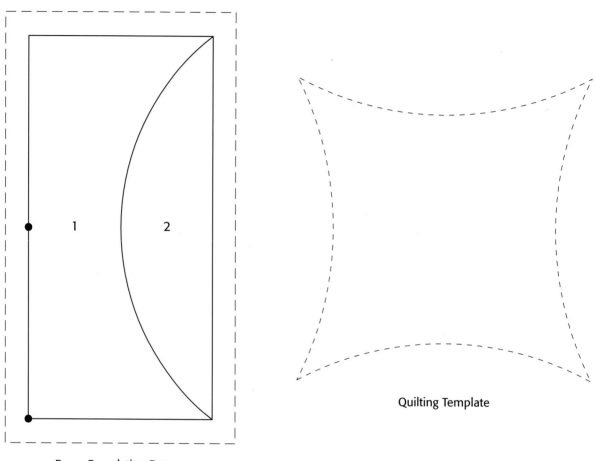

Paper Foundation Pattern

Quilting Template

Crescent Moon Dance

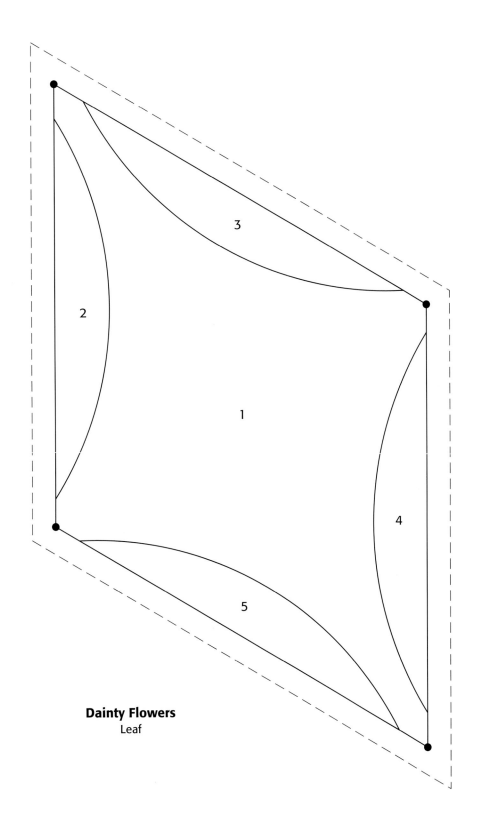

Dainty Flowers
Leaf

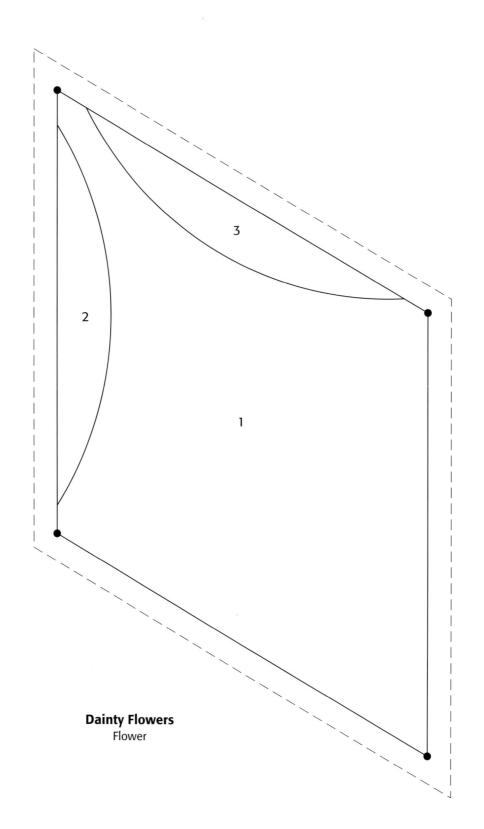

Dainty Flowers
Flower

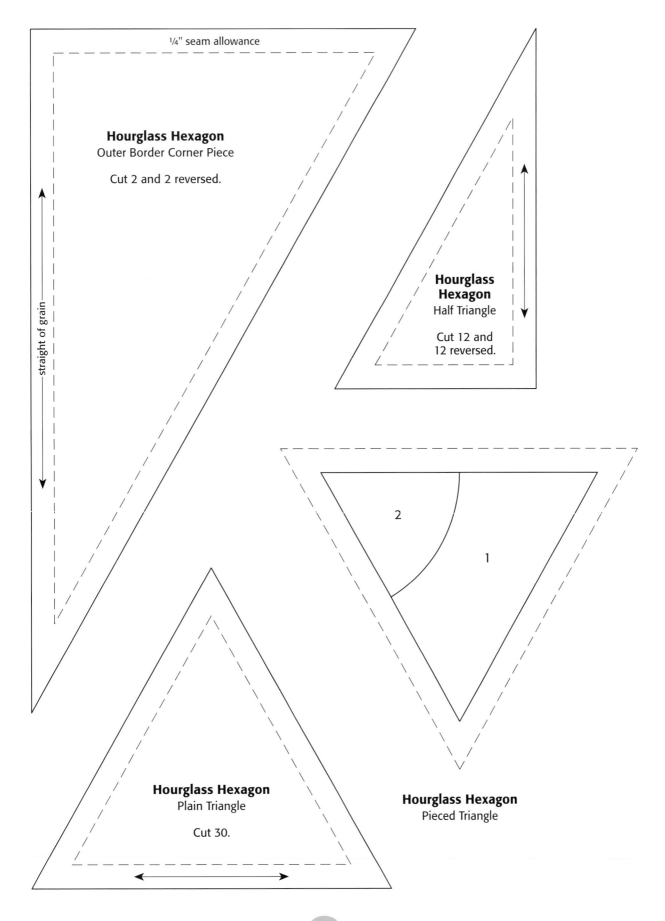

¼" seam allowance

Hourglass Hexagon
Outer Border Corner Piece

Cut 2 and 2 reversed.

straight of grain

Hourglass Hexagon
Half Triangle

Cut 12 and
12 reversed.

2

1

Hourglass Hexagon
Plain Triangle

Cut 30.

Hourglass Hexagon
Pieced Triangle

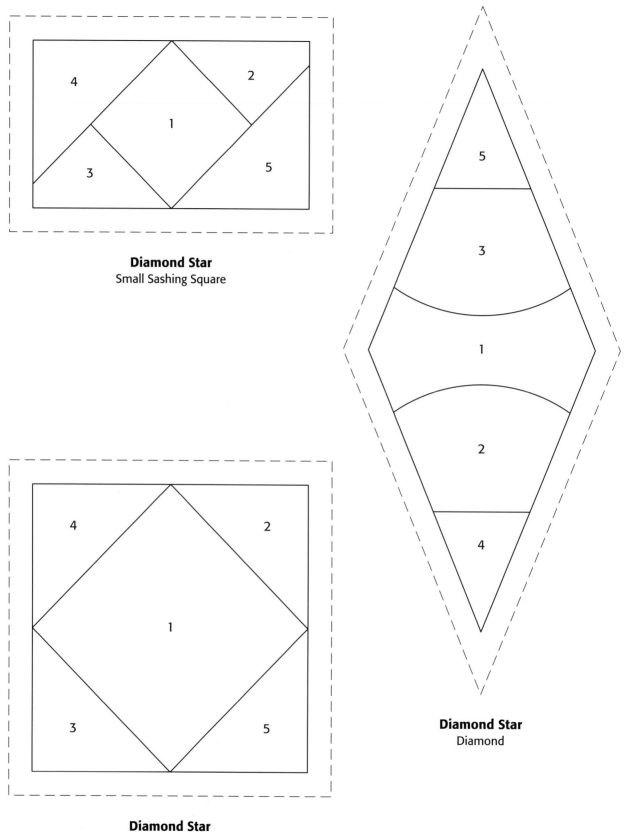

Diamond Star
Small Sashing Square

Diamond Star
Large Sashing Square

Diamond Star
Diamond

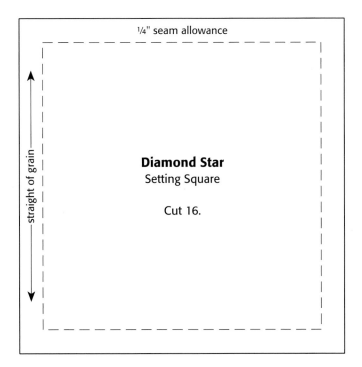

¼" seam allowance

straight of grain

Diamond Star
Setting Square

Cut 16.

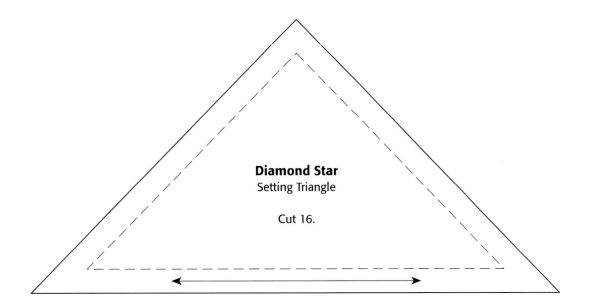

Diamond Star
Setting Triangle

Cut 16.

Resources

NOTHING BEATS VISITING a quilt shop to see all the latest sewn samples and to admire the enticing new fabrics. Believe me, I help the local shops thrive. But there are never enough fabrics and quilting goodies for my appetite, so I often use mail-order and online quilting resources or services. Now I am sharing those resources with you, and I recommend each of them without hesitation.

When shopping for fabric online, I print out a picture of the fabric swatches so that I have a visual record of what I ordered. Then I staple the printout to my quilt design so that I remember exactly how I intended to use the fabric(s) in the quilt.

Big Horn Quilts

529 Greybull Ave.
PO Box 566
Greybull, WY 82426
(877) 586-9150
http://www.bighornquilts.com

Fabric takes center stage on this Web site, and lots of it is at I-can't-resist prices.

Connecting Threads

PO Box 8940
Vancouver, WA 98668-8940
(800) 574-6454

Books and patterns take center stage in this catalog. A selection of rulers, rotary cutters, and other quilting supplies are available, all at discounted prices. Call or write for a free catalog.

eQuilter.com

4581 Maple Court
Boulder, CO 80301
(303) 516-1615
http://www.eQuilter.com

Specializing in Asian-Pacific and contemporary fabrics, eQuilter.com owner Luana Rubin worked throughout Asia as a textile and fashion designer and now brings her love of Asian textiles home to American quilters through her Web site.

Hancock's of Paducah

3841 Hinkleville Road
Paducah, KY 42001
(800) 845-8723
http://www.Hancocks-Paducah.com

Hancock's of Paducah offers a delicious selection of the latest fabrics from the best manufacturers and designers, plus threads, quilting gadgets, batting, and more—all at great prices. Check out both the online catalog and mail-order catalog; one may have fabrics that the other doesn't. Call, write, or visit the Web site to request a free catalog.

Keepsake Quilting

Route 25B
PO Box 1618
Centre Harbor, NH 03226-1618
(800) 865-9458
http://www.keepsakequilting.com

This hefty little catalog is chock-full of quilt notions, gadgets, patterns, books, and fabric, as well as handy Fabric Medleys. No wonder it is entitled, "The Quilter's Wishbook." Call, write, or visit the Web site to request a free catalog.

Pine Tree Quiltworks, Ltd.

585 Broadway
South Portland, ME 04106
(207) 799-7357
http://www.pinetree.quiltworks.com

Pine Tree Quiltworks, Ltd. offers everything a quilter needs, including a wonderful selection of fabrics, and every ruler and notion imaginable—all at discounted prices. Call, write, or visit the Web site to request a free catalog.

Quilt-a-way Fabrics

PO Box 163
Westminster Station, VT 05159
(802) 722-4743
http://www.quiltaway.com

A full-service quilt shop, Quilt-a-way's mail-order Web site offers a great selection of fabrics at low prices, including many batiks.

Quilts and Other Comforts

B2500
Louisiana, MO 63353-7500
(800) 881-6624
http://www.quiltsonline.com

"The catalog for quilt lovers" focuses on fabrics and patterns, with a good selection of popular books and wonderful quilt tools. Some nice gift-type items are featured as well. Call or visit the Web site to order a catalog.

THE FOLLOWING ARE *a few starting points for exploring quilting and foundation piecing in the wonderful world of cyberspace.*

About.com

http://quilting.about.com

The mission of About.com is to be **the** place to go to learn about any topic. Each area is devoted to a specific interest and is hosted by a real, live, accessible human being. The quilting area, hosted by Susan Druding, is a resource for all facets of quilting, offering how-to directions, answers to frequently asked questions, sources, links to other sites, and much more.

Judy Smith's Quilting, Needlearts and Antiques Page

http://www.quiltart.com/judy

Judy is an online quilter who has used the Internet for a long time and has a highly acclaimed site of great quilting links. Start your search with Judy's site, and you will quickly accrue a long list of bookmarked favorites!

Missing Fabrics

http://www.missingfabrics.com

The Missing Fabrics page works! I ran out of fabric for a quilt that started as a wall hanging and then I decided it had to be large enough for a bed. Because it had been produced two seasons before, no local or online shops had any of the fabric. So, I scanned it and posted it on the Missing Fabrics page. Lo and behold a quilter in Canada spotted it on the site and sent her friend, who lived closer to town, to fetch me some of the fabric from their local quilt shop.

PC Piecers

http://bankswith.apollotrust.com/~larryb/
PCPiecers.htm

Dedicated specifically to foundation piecing, the PC Piecers site has a lot of great information, patterns, and activities, as well as links to many other foundation-piecing sites and goodies.

Zippy Designs Publishing
Home of the *Foundation Piecer* Magazine

Rural Route 1, Box 187M
Newport, VA 24128
(888) 544-7153
http://www.zippydesigns.com

This magazine is devoted exclusively to foundation piecing. The creation of husband-and-wife team Elizabeth Schwartz and Stephen Seifert, the *Foundation Piecer* is a full-color magazine filled with inspiring patterns. Published six times a year, each issue contains eight to twelve projects.

The Web site for Zippy Designs is another great resource. Find foundation-piecing instructions, block patterns, information about the magazine and products, and much more at this site.

About the Author

JODIE DAVIS has been designing and sharing her designs for the last twelve years through the more than twenty books she has written. She counts herself as truly lucky to work in the quilting world, which she proclaims is the only real world she believes in.

Martingale & Company
Toll-free: 1-800-426-3126

International: 1-425-483-3313
24-Hour Fax: 1-425-486-7596

PO Box 118, Bothell, WA 98041-0118 USA

Web site: www.patchwork.com
E-mail: info@martingale-pub.com

Books from

These books are available through your local quilt, fabric, craft-supply, or art-supply store. For more information, contact us for a free full-color catalog. You can also find our full catalog of books online at www.patchwork.com.

Appliqué

Appliqué for Baby
Appliqué in Bloom
Baltimore Bouquets
Basic Quiltmaking Techniques for Hand Appliqué
Basic Quiltmaking Techniques for Machine Appliqué
Coxcomb Quilt
The Easy Art of Appliqué
Folk Art Animals
Fun with Sunbonnet Sue
Garden Appliqué
The Nursery Rhyme Quilt
Red and Green: An Appliqué Tradition
Rose Sampler Supreme
Stars in the Garden
Sunbonnet Sue All Through the Year

Beginning Quiltmaking

Basic Quiltmaking Techniques for Borders & Bindings
Basic Quiltmaking Techniques for Curved Piecing
Basic Quiltmaking Techniques for Divided Circles
Basic Quiltmaking Techniques for Eight-Pointed Stars
Basic Quiltmaking Techniques for Hand Appliqué
Basic Quiltmaking Techniques for Machine Appliqué
Basic Quiltmaking Techniques for Strip Piecing
The Quilter's Handbook
Your First Quilt Book (or it should be!)

Crafts

15 Beads
Fabric Mosaics
Folded Fabric Fun
Making Memories

Cross-Stitch & Embroidery

Hand-Stitched Samplers from I Done My Best
Kitties to Stitch and Quilt: 15 Redwork Designs
Miniature Baltimore Album Quilts
A Silk-Ribbon Album

Designing Quilts

Color: The Quilter's Guide
Design Essentials: The Quilter's Guide
Design Your Own Quilts
Designing Quilts: The Value of Value
The Nature of Design
QuiltSkills
Sensational Settings
Surprising Designs from Traditional Quilt Blocks
Whimsies & Whynots

Holiday

Christmas Ribbonry
Easy Seasonal Wall Quilts
Favorite Christmas Quilts from That Patchwork Place
Holiday Happenings
Quilted for Christmas
Quilted for Christmas, Book IV
Special-Occasion Table Runners
Welcome to the North Pole

Home Decorating

The Home Decorator's Stamping Book
Make Room for Quilts
Special-Occasion Table Runners
Stitch & Stencil
Welcome Home: Debbie Mumm
Welcome Home: Kaffe Fassett

Knitting

Simply Beautiful Sweaters
Two Sticks and a String

Paper Arts

The Art of Handmade Paper and Collage
Grow Your Own Paper
Stamp with Style

Paper Piecing

Classic Quilts with Precise Foundation Piecing
Easy Machine Paper Piecing
Easy Mix & Match Machine Paper Piecing
Easy Paper-Pieced Keepsake Quilts
Easy Paper-Pieced Miniatures
Easy Reversible Vests
Go Wild with Quilts
Go Wild with Quilts—Again!
It's Raining Cats & Dogs
Mariner's Medallion
Needles and Notions
Paper-Pieced Curves
Paper Piecing the Seasons
A Quilter's Ark
Sewing on the Line
Show Me How to Paper Piece

Quilting & Finishing Techniques

The Border Workbook
Borders by Design
A Fine Finish
Happy Endings
Interlacing Borders
Lap Quilting Lives!
Loving Stitches
Machine Quilting Made Easy
Quilt It!
Quilting Design Sourcebook
Quilting Makes the Quilt
The Ultimate Book of Quilt Labels

Ribbonry

Christmas Ribbonry
A Passion for Ribbonry
Wedding Ribbonry

Rotary Cutting & Speed Piecing

101 Fabulous Rotary-Cut Quilts
365 Quilt Blocks a Year Perpetual Calendar
All-Star Sampler
Around the Block with Judy Hopkins
Basic Quiltmaking Techniques for Strip Piecing
Beyond Log Cabin
Block by Block
Easy Stash Quilts
Fat Quarter Quilts
The Joy of Quilting
A New Twist on Triangles
A Perfect Match
Quilters on the Go
ScrapMania
Shortcuts
Simply Scrappy Quilts
Spectacular Scraps
Square Dance
Stripples Strikes Again!
Strips That Sizzle
Surprising Designs from Traditional Quilt Blocks

Traditional Quilts with Painless Borders
Time-Crunch Quilts
Two-Color Quilts

Small & Miniature Quilts

Bunnies by the Bay Meets Little Quilts
Celebrate! With Little Quilts
Easy Paper-Pieced Miniatures
Fun with Miniature Log Cabin Blocks
Little Quilts all Through the House
Living with Little Quilts
Miniature Baltimore Album Quilts
A Silk-Ribbon Album
Small Quilts Made Easy
Small Wonders

Surface Design

Complex Cloth
Creative Marbling on Fabric
Dyes & Paints
Fantasy Fabrics
Hand-Dyed Fabric Made Easy
Jazz It Up
Machine Quilting with Decorative Threads
New Directions in Chenille
Thread Magic
Threadplay with Libby Lehman

Topics in Quiltmaking

Bargello Quilts
The Cat's Meow
Even More Quilts for Baby
Everyday Angels in Extraordinary Quilts
Fabric Collage Quilts
Fast-and-Fun Stenciled Quilts
Folk Art Quilts
It's Raining Cats & Dogs
Kitties to Stitch and Quilt: 15 Redwork Designs
Life in the Country with Country Threads
Machine-Stitched Cathedral Windows
More Quilts for Baby
A New Slant on Bargello Quilts
Patchwork Pantry
Pink Ribbon Quilts
Quilted Landscapes
The Quilted Nursery
Quilting Your Memories
Quilts for Baby
Quilts from Aunt Amy
Whimsies & Whynots

Watercolor Quilts

More Strip-Pieced Watercolor Magic
Quick Watercolor Quilts
Strip-Pieced Watercolor Magic
Watercolor Impressions
Watercolor Quilts

Wearables

Easy Reversible Vests
Just Like Mommy
New Directions in Chenille
Quick-Sew Fleece
Variations in Chenille

1/0